WHAT IS THE REASON?

by Dru Hunter

CREATIVE EDUCATION • CREATIVE PAPERBACKS

Published by **Creative Education** and **Creative Paperbacks**
P.O. Box 227, Mankato, Minnesota 56002
Creative Education and Creative Paperbacks are imprints of The Creative Company
www.thecreativecompany.us

Design and production by **Christine Vanderbeek**
Art direction by **Rita Marshall**
Printed in Malaysia

Photographs by Alamy (AF archive, avatra images, dbimages, Randy Duchaine,
Pictorial Press Ltd, Steve Vidler, Carol and Mike Werner), Corbis (Bettmann, Frederic
Cirou/PhotoAlto, ClassicStock, Corbis, David Lees, FRED PROUSER/Reuters, Mark
Richards/ZUMA Press, Science Photo Library, Ronald Siemoneit/Sygma, Tarker,
Dadang Tri/Reuters, Ken Welsh/*/Design Pics, JENS WOLF/epa), Getty Images
(Bloomberg, Mike Powell, SLADE Paul), iStockphoto (imgendesign), Newscom
(Disney Pixar/ZUMAPRESS, World History Archive), Shutterstock (Dragon Images,
Fisherss, Georgios Kollidas, Thammasak Lek, Marzolino, Dudarev Mikhail, Marina Sun)

Library of Congress Cataloging-in-Publication Data
Hunter, Dru.
What is the reason? / Dru Hunter.
p. cm. — (Think like a scientist)
Includes bibliographical references and index.
Summary: A narration of the origins, advancements, and future of the formal
sciences, including mathematics and computer science, and the ways in which
scientists utilize the scientific method to explore questions.

ISBN 978-1-60818-595-5 (hardcover)
ISBN 978-1-62832-200-2 (pbk)
1. Science—Methodology—Juvenile literature. 2. Scientists—Juvenile literature. 3.
Information science—Juvenile literature. I. Title.

Q175.2.H867 2015
500—dc23   2014033140

CCSS: RI.5.1, 2, 3, 8; RI.6.1, 3, 7; RST.6-8.1, 2, 5, 6, 8

First Edition HC 9 8 7 6 5 4 3 2 1
First Edition PBK 9 8 7 6 5 4 3 2 1

ON THE COVER 19th-century English mathematician Ada Lovelace

TABLE OF CONTENTS

SCIENTIST IN THE SPOTLIGHT

INTRODUCTION

During World War II, the Nazis sent secret codes to their military officers about war tactics. The Allies—such as Great Britain and the United States—attempted to break those codes because lives and the fate of the world were at stake.

The Allies were up against the Germans' Enigma machine, which looked like a typewriter but could turn ordinary messages into an encrypted code. Because no letter in the code was repeated, normal codebreaking methods did not apply. British mathematician Alan Turing was working furiously alongside other scientists to break the Enigma codes. In 1939, he helped design a decryption machine that was used in cracking the settings behind the Enigma. The Allies could now break Nazi codes in 20 minutes!

Reason is the ability of the mind to make sense of what is going on through logic. Mathematicians such as Turing

look for patterns. They think about all the different ways to arrive at an answer. Computer science is a relatively new field with roots in the mathematical calculations of the 1800s. By applying math, computer scientists develop methods of computing or processing information. Mathematicians and computer scientists use their math and science knowledge to investigate and their reason to solve problems in a logical way. Whether it is coming up with a code to protect a bank account or calculating a submarine's safe journey to the bottom of the ocean and back, decision-making systems all rely on the ability to reason.

HISTORY OF NUMBERS

A 37,000-YEAR-OLD BABOON BONE WITH 27 ETCHES across it was found in Swaziland in the 1970s. Scientists think it is one of the oldest examples of people doing math. Just like the other sciences, mathematics came about because of the needs of people. Primitive, or early, people did not have much need for math beyond the ability to count things. However, as societies became more complex and looked to build temples, accumulate wealth, and explore or conquer, they required mathematicians to advance math beyond simple counting. New mathematical methods were needed to solve increasingly complicated problems.

Computations have been discovered on artifacts from many different cultures across the globe. Our knowledge of the early Babylonians' and Sumerians' math comes from clay tablets dating from more than 3,000 years ago. The early mathematicians wrote on tablets while the clay was still moist and then baked them in the sun's heat. Operations such as

The Babylonian math tablets used the cuneiform writing system.

multiplication, division, fractions, and algebra have been found on those tablets. One of the ancient tablets even looked like graded math homework.

Scientists have an understanding of what the ancient Egyptians knew about math from the Rhind, Moscow, and Berlin papyruses, which date from the 1800s to the 1600s B.C. The Rhind papyrus included instructions on how to do geometry. On the Moscow papyrus were math word problems and how to solve them. The Berlin papyrus showed the Egyptians doing algebraic equations.

While some ancient civilizations left behind evidence of what they understood about math, others—such as many native North American tribes—left no trace. We do not know what math they understood and applied to build their structures, some of which still survive today. In other ancient societies, such as early China, math was taught by spoken word. The Chou Pei Suan Ching, or *The Arithmetical Classic of the Gnomon and the Circular Paths of Heaven*, is the earliest known Chinese mathematical text and dates to approximately 200 B.C. Some of the mathematical findings show Chinese math as being very different compared with the rest of the world from around the same time. This has led many scientists to believe Chinese math developed independently from math elsewhere.

The ancient civilization of the Mycenaeans (circa 1900–1100 B.C.) is considered the start of Greek culture in what is now modern mainland Greece and a group of islands. The roots of the **scientific method** used today by scientists began with Greek philosopher Thales of Miletus (620–526 B.C.). By the 300s B.C., Greek mathematicians were spread across the empire into the Middle East and northern Africa.

Thales of Miletus (below) reportedly used math to figure out the height of Giza's Great Pyramid (opposite).

CHARLES BABBAGE

English mathematician and inventor Charles Babbage (1791–1871) was often sick as a child, so he had to receive most of his early education at home. His tutors and other teachers encouraged his study of math. He graduated from Cambridge University and later became a professor of mathematics at his former university in 1828. It was during the 1820s that he began working on a mathematical machine called the difference engine. His more complex analytical engine invention (shown above) is often credited as the forerunner of the modern computer. It was designed to do math as well as to save data and perform other basic functions like today's computers. The tools Babbage needed to make his analytical engine did not exist, and he applied for government funding to help pay for the project. His designs did not become a full reality until they were constructed—and proven to work—more than 100 years after his death.

They shared a common language and worshiped the same gods, and during this time, mathematics thrived. Euclid, a Greek mathematician who lived in Alexandria, Egypt, around 300 B.C., wrote *Elements*, considered one of the most influential and important books in the advancement of mathematics.

Euclid's *Elements* consists of 13 books that define geometry and geometric algebra. Euclid came up with several **theorems** and ways to prove them, including how to find the square root of a number. Alexandria was the center of mathematics until fires from civil wars and conquests destroyed its library between 48 B.C. and A.D. 642. Greek math was further developed by Persians such as Muhammad ibn Musa al-Khwarizmi, who is often called the "Father of Algebra"— just as Euclid was called the "Father of Geometry." The invention of the printing press enabled Euclid's *Elements* to be mass-produced. It became the standard geometry textbook until the 1900s.

The ancient Sumerians and Greeks were also among the first to use mechanical devices for math. Their devices provided the roots of computer science. The Sumerian abacus dates back to around 2500 B.C. and was used for counting on a number system with a base of 60. The later innovations of Greek and Egyptian abacuses would move stones on tablets of metal.

Today, people around the world may still employ an abacus for counting operations or teaching math.

In 1900, a group of sponge divers discovered the wreck of an ancient cargo ship off the Greek island of Antikythera. They retrieved from the ruins artifacts such as marble statues, jewelry, coins, and a contraption that would later be named the Antikythera Mechanism. The device went unnoticed at the National Museum of Archeology in Athens for two years. The scientists had been so busy analyzing other artifacts that when they finally turned their attention to the corroded lump of bronze, they were astounded.

Once the device was cleaned up, its 2,000-plus inscriptions and

DID YOU KNOW? Fellow English mathematician Ada Lovelace made the first **algorithm** for Charles Babbage's analytical engine and is considered the world's first computer programmer.

80 fragmented pieces could be seen. Apart from theorizing that the device had been mounted in a wooden frame, scientists didn't understand much about the workings of this ancient Greek computer until 2006. Then, by using three-dimensional X-rays, they were able to reconstruct the machine and found 30 different gears inside it. High-resolution surface imaging provided visibility of the almost vanished surface writings. The results dated the Antikythera Mechanism to approximately 150–87 B.C., and the early computer was so advanced that nothing like it was built for a thousand years.

In the late 1600s, Gottfried Wilhelm von Leibniz, a German mathematician and philosopher, came up with calculus, a mathematical study of the rates of change, as in accelerations. (English mathematician Isaac Newton was also investigating the same thing at the time.) Leibniz invented a calculating machine that could add and subtract as well as divide and multiply. He discovered the binary system, which uses only the numerals zero and one.

Modern computers run on that binary system, and the inventor of the first computer, Charles Babbage, considered using binary code to run his difference engine in 1821. However, Babbage opted instead to use decimal math—numerals from zero to nine—to reduce the number of moving parts in his machine. Babbage saw only partial sections of his invention completed in his lifetime.

The calculations needed to hurl missiles, drop bombs, and fire artillery during war were what furthered the development of computers. While working toward a doctoral degree at Harvard in the late 1930s, Howard Aiken designed an electromechanical computer. The company IBM agreed to build it, and in 1944, the machine returned to Harvard as the Mark I. The U.S. Navy put it to use right away, and Aiken began working on other Mark computers alongside programmer Grace Hopper.

Compared with today's computers, the Mark I was loud, massive in scale, and slow. The computer filled an entire large room with its 51 feet (15.5 m) in length and 8 feet (2.4 m) in ceiling height. Weighing 5 tons (4.5 t), it was made of more than 750,000 electronic units and produced very loud, metallic-pounding clicks. It took about five seconds for it to do a multiplication problem, but it could perform all the other basic arithmetic functions, including addition, subtraction, and division. Capable of transmitting data on its 500 miles (805 km) of wire and 1,464 switches, it could also do higher math such as **trigonometry** and take numbers to 23 decimal places. The computer's results were outputted to an electric typewriter. The Mark I showed how a machine could do calculations without error, inspiring other scientists to invent smaller, faster computers able to handle more complex tasks, which in turn furthered the field of computer science.

Pieces of the Mark I computer (once comprising 750,000 parts) are displayed at Harvard's Science Center.

TRY IT OUT! Math problems can be answered by the Internet. Using the search bar in your computer's Internet browser (such as Google), type in this math problem: "What is 9769 plus 2365?" Hit "return," and see if the right answer appears!

SURF THE NET

THE COMPUTER'S DEVELOPMENT SINCE THE ANCIENT Greeks' Antikythera Mechanism is the result of many inventors. Computers are complex machines. All the mechanical parts of the computer—as well as the languages used to make it perform—have required new inventions.

Back in 1961, computers were not in most households as they are today. A computer at that time was four times larger than a kitchen stove and, when powered on, sounded like a weed whacker. Not to mention that it cost more than $100,000 to own one. The only places most computers could be found were on college campuses.

To convince more people to buy and use computers, Massachusetts Institute of Technology (MIT) computer scientists Peter Samson and Steve Russell invented the first computer game—*Spacewar!*—in 1961. The game involved two players battling against each other in spaceships around a star. The developers said one of the challenges they

Over the years, computers have become increasingly widespread—and portable.

faced was the limited processor technology, which made it difficult to translate the actions of each player's movement in real time. Most players of the first video game were computer programmers, and new versions of *Spacewar!* would appear because others were taking the work and changing it without permission. "You couldn't copyright software in those days," Samson says.

Samson's second version of the game kept score and showed explosions. Other computer scientists added mines, invisible spaceships, and cockpit views. The game became more popular, and companies such as IBM were having problems with their employees playing the game while at work. Even though *Spacewar!* is more than 50 years old, Samson points out that it has "no outstanding user complaints, no catastrophic crashes, and it's still available."

Three years after the invention of the first video game, American engineer Dr. Douglas Engelbart made something most of us now use every day. Engelbart founded one of the research centers at the Stanford Research Institute (SRI). In 1964, SRI received a **patent** for a device with two metal wheels and a wooden shell that Engelbart called the "X-Y position indicator for a display system." It was nicknamed the "mouse" because the wire came out the end like a tail. Engelbart is credited with making computers easier for most people to operate. Computers were not just for specially trained scientists anymore.

By the time of his death in 2013, Engelbart had more than 45 patents to his name. But some innovations, such as his digital workspace programs for what is now called Windows, went unpatented because of rules in place during that time regarding patent application. His other contributions to computer science included teleconferencing, and he was involved in the early development of the Internet. In

The sleek modern mouse (opposite) was patterned after Engelbart's version (below) with rolling wheels.

FLORENCE NIGHTINGALE

Florence Nightingale (1820–1910) was a British war nurse who made important contributions to mathematics. A gifted math student since childhood, during the 1850s Crimean War against Russia, she tracked the causes of deaths and discovered that most of the casualties were the result of poor hospital sanitation. Nightingale wanted to persuade British government officials to improve hygiene and cleanliness in hospitals but decided telling them the raw statistics might not be enough. So she developed a kind of pie chart she called "coxcombs," which is now known as the polar area diagram. She used similar statistics-based practices to report on sanitation conditions in India, which was then part of the British Empire. Nightingale's statistical pie charts helped change policies that then saved lives. In 1858, she became the first woman elected to the Royal Statistical Society.

1968, he demonstrated the first videoconference by having a conversation with a colleague who was 31 miles (50 km) away. His theory of how pages of data could be strung together by using links is how the World Wide Web was later made. Apple Computer **licensed** Engelbart's computer mouse from SRI for $40,000 in 1983 as the personal computer Lisa made its debut.

Widespread Internet usage began in the 1990s, but the technology itself is much older. A computer network called ARPANET (Advanced Research Projects Agency Network), after the group known as ARPA, was developed in 1966. ARPA hosted a program called Resource Sharing Networks with other research agencies to link computers together. The U.S. government was looking for a way to protect information yet be able to distribute it in the event of a disaster such as a nuclear strike.

The **acoustical** consulting company Bolt, Beranek and Newman (BBN) won the government contract to create ARPANET. Its team was made up of computer scientists, engineers, and mathematicians. The first four computers in the network belonged to the University of California, Los Angeles; the Stanford Research Institute; the Culler-Fried Interactive Mathematics Center of the University of California, Santa Barbara; and the University of Utah. On the first attempt to connect, the system crashed. But once it was up and running, scientists could harness the computers' collective power.

An early router called the Interface Message Processor helped UCLA send ARPANET's first message in 1969.

The ARPANET team had to invent each computer process as needed. From logging into the system to moving files between machines, the string of obstacles the scientists had to navigate was seemingly endless. The numeric host addresses they developed became what we use today as domain names.

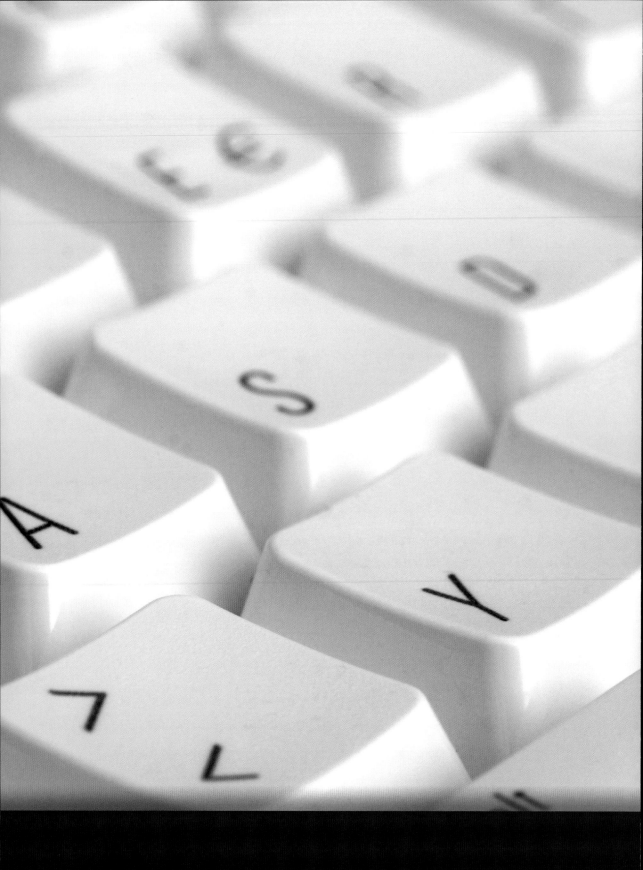

DID YOU KNOW? The average American adult spends about 60 hours a month on the computer, which is equivalent to 30 days a year.

ARPANET was one of the first early networks to send data through a process called packet switching, which allowed computers to break down files into individual fragments called packets. After transfer, the packets reassembled into their original form. Packet switching enabled data to travel at higher speeds compared with the previous technology of message switching, in which the whole message was sent at once, stored, and then forwarded.

By 1977, ARPANET consisted of more than 100 university, research center, and military computers. With ARPANET, people were now able to use a computer to sign into another across the country. Information from another computer could be accessed and transferred without having to travel to get it. Computer programmer Ray Tomlinson of BBN designed an early version of e-mail for use on ARPANET. He was the first to use the "@" symbol in e-mail. Satellites connected computers to overseas machines in Hawaii and Europe. The U.S. military left ARPANET in 1983 in favor of its own internal network. Three years later, other networks began to join together to make larger ones, and the system soon became referred to as "the Internet." In 1990, the plug was pulled on ARPANET because it had met its goal. (It had actually exceeded what it set out to do.) Because of ARPANET, U.S. citizens could now receive and transfer data nationwide as well as worldwide.

Companies such as IBM and Apple began making the first consumer computers in the 1970s. Bill Gates, cofounder of Microsoft Corporation, announced in 1983 the company would make its Windows operating system with a graphical user interface (GUI) for IBM computers. Apple's Lisa and Macintosh computers already came equipped with GUI. Despite several legal battles with Apple over copyright issues in the next few years, Microsoft became the top software company in 1988.

One of the reasons some consumer computer companies, such as Processor Technology and Eagle Computer, failed while Apple and Microsoft succeeded had to do with program development. Consumers decided that computers with more options—meaning more programs and applications—were worth purchasing. Most computer software today is made for use with both Mac and Windows-based computers.

Computer programmers usually work in groups to develop software. Some of the most popular computer software programs allow people to do their own taxes, make their own greeting cards, write resumes, and learn new languages. Computer games for education as well as entertainment have evolved since the days of *Spacewar!* Some of 2014's top computer games, according to *PC Gamer Magazine*, were *Portal* by Valve Corporation and *World of Warcraft* by Blizzard Entertainment. Computer science has changed the ways in which businesses operate, students learn, people communicate, and audiences view entertainment.

Apple's 2010 release of the iPad represented a new era in the computing and communications industries.

TRY IT OUT! Make a pie chart to show the percentage or fraction of what school subjects your classmates like best. The whole pie chart should equal 100 percent. Include a title and key to describe what the colors or portions represent.

LIGHTS! CAMERA! CGI!

BEFORE COMPUTERS, MOVIE MONSTERS WERE MADE of plastic or based on people wearing rubber suits. Settings that took place on other worlds had to be made inside a movie studio with materials that could be found or constructed. Real explosions and fires had to be set. Pencils were used to draw cartoons. Because of computers, there is a big visual difference between a film made just 20 years ago and one released today.

Computer-generated imagery (CGI) can add fire effects to a burning boat. It can change a day scene into night. A crowd of 5 people can be made to look like 500. CGI gives filmmakers the ability to do almost anything they can think of and make it look amazing and real. Matte painting is a production effect where digital matte painters use photographs, 3-D models, and animation to create grand images, such as an explosion in a James Bond film or the mystical landscapes in *Avatar*. Today, computers can be used

The acclaimed Toy Story movies showed the possibilities of computer animation.

for almost every aspect of a film. From the screenplay, budget, **storyboarding**, and previewing to editing the captured footage and watching the completed project, computers and the scientists behind the software make it happen.

Frank Vitz does computer-generated effects for movies and worked on the 1982 Disney film *Tron*, the first live-action movie to use a lot of CGI and animation. Though computers are common today, most people did not know much about them in the '80s. And there weren't many computer scientists who knew how to create visual effects using computers. Vitz and a few others took on the challenge to make the groundbreaking film. In a 2011 interview for *Computer Graphics World*, Vitz noted that the film was revolutionary because the team needed to invent any tools it needed, "including models and miniatures, motion control, cell animation, live action, rotoscoping, optical compositing, and the brand-new computer graphics systems."

Another film that was a pioneer of computer-generated visual effects was 1980's *Star Wars: The Empire Strikes Back*. When director George Lucas began production on the Star Wars movies, he wanted them to have special effects never before seen on film. To achieve this, he started his own visual effects company in 1975, Industrial Light and Magic (ILM), and hired computer scientists, engineers, and artists. Since making the computer-generated effects for the Star Wars films, ILM has created special effects for nearly 300 movies, including such series as Harry Potter, Jurassic Park, and Indiana Jones.

From the Star Wars (opposite) to Jurassic Park (below) franchises, ILM's effects created a buzz.

In 1989, ILM used computer-generated effects on water for the first time. The science-fiction plot of *The Abyss* is about finding

ARISTOTLE

The Greek philosopher Aristotle was born in 384 B.C. and was the tutor of the future conqueror and king Alexander the Great. Aristotle taught that logic was the way we could understand anything. He created rules to follow for correct reasoning and making sound arguments. According to Aristotle, if you want to understand something, you should first think about it in terms of its characteristics and categories. Then use deduction to gather information. In starting his own school in Athens called the Lyceum, Aristotle amassed one of the greatest libraries of the time. It was filled with manuscripts on math and science and every subject in between. Of Aristotle's own writings, only about 6 percent of an estimated 200 works are still in circulation. He instructed his students to ask why and look for proof, once writing, "We do not have knowledge of a thing until we have grasped its why, that is to say, its cause."

extraterrestrial life as the navy tries to recover a lost nuclear submarine. ILM designed a program to create different-sized surface waves
that would be used to show a creature emerging from the depths.
It took 6 months to generate the 75 seconds of computer graphics.
At the Academy Awards, *The Abyss* won for Best Visual Effects. By
the time the 2000 movie *The Perfect Storm* was released, an entire
ocean could be digitally created.

The first feature film to be entirely computer animated was
Pixar's *Toy Story* in 1995. Pixar's team used arithmetic, geometry, and
trigonometry as they invented math programs for the computer to
bring characters such as Woody and Buzz to life. Before he worked
on Pixar films such as *Toy Story 2*, Tony DeRose was a professor of
computer science researching computer graphics. "I can't remem-
ber a time when I wasn't interested in science, but my
interest in mathematics really began when I was in
seventh grade," DeRose has said. His favorite character
to animate was Geri from the short film *Geri's Game.*
"He was the first character I worked on, and he won an
Oscar," said DeRose. "He also made a cameo appear-
ance in *Toy Story 2* as the toy cleaner." DeRose tells
people who want to make computer-generated movies
that they should "learn as much mathematics as you
can, particularly applied math. The areas of mathematics we use
most heavily today are Euclidean and affine geometry, trigonometry,
linear algebra, calculus, and numerical analysis. We don't really know
what the mathematical tools of tomorrow might be, so we're counting on the next generation of employees to tell us." DeRose says
his favorite part about his work is "solving problems that have never
been solved before."

Apple's cofounder Steve Jobs helped design the Pixar building

*Although computer-
animated, the incredibly life-
like characters in* Toy Story
resonated with viewers.

DID YOU KNOW? Computer scientists often work with biologists, environmental scientists, and oceanographers to study the planet and its living things.

Even fantasy worlds and characters (such as Gollum, above) contain elements based on biological fact.

with special purposes in mind. People who develop the computer software code work in one area, while the animators and designers work in another section. However, all the meeting rooms, bathrooms, and cafeteria are in the center. This makes it so that everyone has to run into each other, which allows them to share information and ideas.

Director Peter Jackson cofounded a computer visual effects company, Weta Digital, in New Zealand. Named after a New Zealand insect, Weta made thousands of computer-generated three-dimensional creatures for the Lord of the Rings movies. Animators combined New Zealand's mountains and forests and used computers to digitally create the fictional setting of Middle Earth. To make the creature Gollum, they used a combination of computer generation, animation, and footage of actor Andy Serkis performing the creature's movements. Inside a studio, Serkis had markers attached to certain locations all over his body. In a technique called motion capture, special cameras recorded the markers as the actor moved, which helped the designers give the animated Gollum more natural movements. In addition, Serkis's legs were digitally altered to make Gollum appear weak.

Motion capture was also used to change actors into the blue-skinned race of Pandora in the 2009 blockbuster movie *Avatar*. The same year *Toy Story* debuted, director James Cameron began working on *Avatar*. He intended to film it with digital effects, but it took more than a decade before he felt computer technology had advanced enough for it to be made. Cameron had to develop new technology with a performance capture camera. Collaborating with Jackson's Weta Digital, the *Avatar* team pushed digital effects technology farther than ever before. Weta had to tweak algorithms in its computer programs to capture the movements and facial expressions Cameron wanted the audience to see on screen, and

such painstaking work took longer than planned. Despite the intense effort involved, most computer animators believe the finished product is worth it and are eager to continue coming up with new innovations. According to Wayne Stables, Weta's digital visual effects supervisor, "So there's the thought that, yes, we will have to push our technology, and yes, it will be challenging, but it's pretty exciting to think about what the results might be."

Cameron's Avatar became the highest-grossing film of all time, earning $2.8 billion at the box office.

TRY IT OUT! For a fun logic game with a friend, have your friend write down a four-digit code. You will have 12 chances to deduce what it is! After each guess, your friend should tell you if anything about the numbers or their order is wrong.

A LOGICAL FUTURE

I N 2000, THE CLAY MATHEMATICS INSTITUTE (CMI) OF Cambridge, Massachusetts, announced a $1-million Millennium Prize for the correct solution to any one of seven problems. The problems were chosen because, after many years of mathematicians working on them, they remained unsolved. The institute wanted to celebrate the new millennium and to make the public aware that there were still opportunities for breakthroughs in math.

One of the problems, known as the Poincaré conjecture, was solved by Russian mathematician Grigori Perelman in 2003. The Poincaré conjecture was first proposed in 1904 by French mathematician Henri Poincaré. It was the most famous math problem in topology, which is the study of geometric shapes and spaces. Perelman impressed the academic world when he proved the conjecture was true, but he shocked everyone when he refused the prize money because of his "disagreement with the organized mathematical community."

Topologists study diagrams of unbroken knots such as the trefoil.

While some mathematicians are hard at work on seemingly un-solvable problems of the past, others are taking a closer look at what past information signifies for challenges of the future. Cliodynamics is a field that combines mathematics and history as scientists search for historical patterns and use data to **hypothesize** expected pro-jections. Using statistical software, some mathematicians have found what they call 100-year waves of instability in such civilizations as Rome, China, medieval England, and even the U.S. **Econophysics** researchers at the New England Complex Systems Institute claim that such instability is caused by trends in food prices. They are col-lecting data and trying to determine if we are about to experience another age of instability.

Historically, instability rang-ing from politics (opposite) to food prices (below) has caused public unrest.

The cost of food goes up when the supply is too small to meet the demand. Researchers believe that supply will fall short of demand in other areas as well, such as computer-related careers. It is estimated that by 2018, there will not be enough college graduates to fill the expected 1.4 million available computer science jobs. As computer scientists today use their skills on a variety of projects, some are even working on ways for computers to help us control things with our minds.

Scientists from the Minnesota College of Science and Engineering have already been able to get five test subjects (three women and two men) to move a quadcopter using the power of their thoughts or electrical brain activity. No wires had to be implanted. The subjects simply wore a hat that was fitted with electrodes, which transmitted voltage changes to a computer when the brain's neurons sent signals. If the computer recognized the transmission, it would move the quadcopter. For example, if the subject made a right fist,

RENE DESCARTES

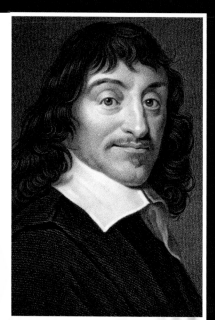

Rene Descartes (1596–1650) was a French mathematician and philosopher. In 1637, he published a book on geometry that proclaimed a new math called analytic geometry. Descartes saw everything in the physical world around him as something that could be explained using math and science. He described the human brain as working like a machine and the universe as a mathematically designed engine—on a very large scale. However, in addition to the physical realm, he believed that reality consisted of a separate mental realm, which meant that the matters of the mind and soul could be taken care of by philosophy and religion. Descartes liked to do most of his thinking in the mornings while still in bed, analyzing his dreams. One of his most famous philosophical statements (written in a book the same year as his geometry work) was, "I think, therefore I am."

possibilities for this type of application in the future, as long as the technology keeps advancing. Thought-powered, computerized devices might even help people move their robotic limbs one day.

As computers are designed to apply to more areas of people's lives, computer scientists continue to refine all the parts of the machine. Silicon is the material computer **transistors** have been made from for the last several decades. The problem with silicon is that as it is used on smaller and smaller transistors, the more it leaks heat. But carbon nanotubes (CNTs) may be able to replace silicon. A complete computer was made of CNTs in the fall of 2013. It is a simple computer, limited to counting and another basic program, but computer scientists believe it will advance into the computer of the future.

Many businesses have made the switch from traditional mainframe computers (pictured) to cloud technology.

The "parts" of computers that cannot be seen—such as where data is stored—are often the most useful to everyday people. Cloud computing is starting to make its presence known, and it may change the entire computer industry. With cloud computing, only one application is loaded, and a central server administers it instead of a person having to install individual software for each computer. The network of remote computers connected in the cloud runs all the applications. E-mail services such as Google's Gmail are examples of cloud computing, as the software for Gmail does not exist on any individual user's computer. The user logs into her Gmail account to access the cloud. Computer scientists who work on cloud devices such as Seagate Central (a type of external hard drive) troubleshoot potential issues, including safeguarding privacy and securing the device.

Issues surrounding privacy and online security are important to many. An estimated 9 million people have their identity stolen each

DID YOU KNOW? After a million comes a billion, trillion, quadrillion, quintillion, sextillion, septillion, octillion, nonillion, decillion, and undecillion.

Above: Engineers unload a tsunami detection buoy in Indonesia.

year. To help combat such theft, mathematicians and computer scientists look for ways people can protect themselves in an increasingly digitized world. A study by Michigan State University researchers found that when computer users installed antivirus, anti-spyware, and anti-adware software, they cut their risk of identity theft in half. Each of the security softwares has a different function in protecting files and keeping the machine secure. Anti-spyware and anti-adware keep programs from installing on your computer without your knowledge or gathering information such as passwords. Antivirus software removes harmful worms and viruses that can steal your files and destroy your data. **Cyberattacks** pose such a threat that computer scientists are always developing powerful new software to protect computer users. The Defense Advanced Research Projects Agency (DARPA) is a worldwide team of supercomputer scientists committed to addressing those concerns.

Mathematicians and computer scientists are also working on computers that can think and react like humans. IBM's cognitive computing division is developing software and computer chips that could someday be installed in search-and-rescue robots that function in places too dangerous for human rescuers to go. Computer buoys floating on the ocean could even warn of oncoming tsunamis.

Cognitive computing machines such as IBM's Watson are designed to learn from and assist humans. The team that built Watson develops software that responds in much the same way as a mathematical scientist would. "The goal is to have computers start to interact in natural human terms ..., understanding the questions that humans ask and providing answers that humans can understand and justify," IBM says. Based on the question asked of it, Watson picks up clues and ranks possible answers, ultimately deciding which is most accurate.

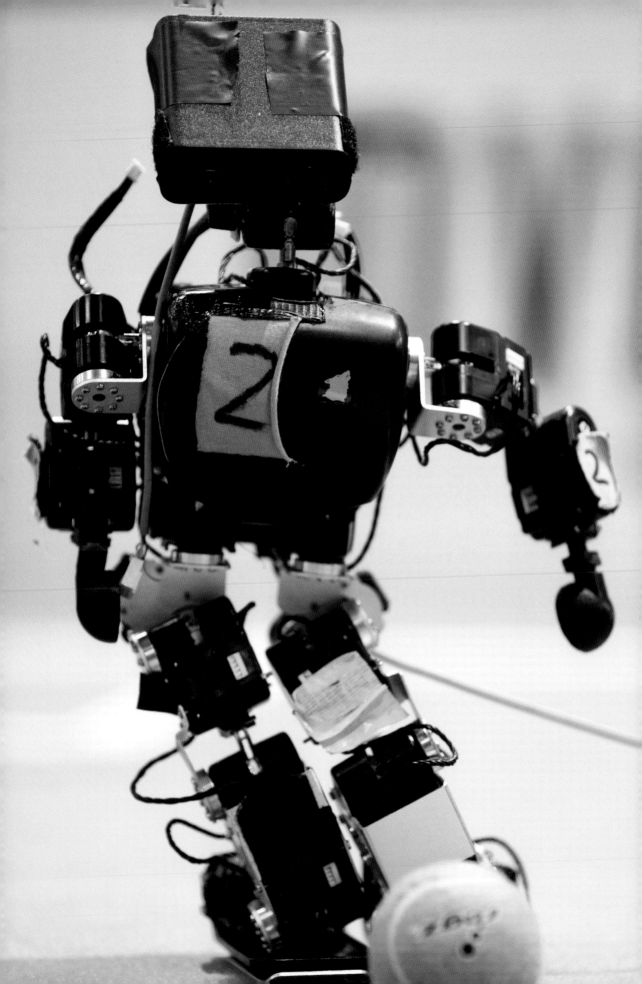

While some scientists are working on computers to aid in medicine, communication, personal security, and national defense, others are designing them for use in transportation. As of 2014, Google had begun building 100 self-driving, electric-powered cars. The only thing the driver controls in these two-seaters is a red button for emergency stops and a start button. The driverless car would pick up its passenger and drive to the destination selected on a smartphone. Some scientists believe that, since the driverless car is already here, the next step is a car that is a big computer. Such vehicles would run by artificial intelligence (AI), communicating with other vehicles while transporting passengers down the road. The big computer would discern when to speed up, slow down, and stop at a red light.

These computer cars may also be driven by AI robots. Robots can already work in assembly lines. Through a computer, AI robots receive information and use stored data to act on that information. The robot can only solve problems and perform actions that it is programmed to do. The main challenge of creating AI robots is that everything has to be invented. Some scientists see a future where humans and intelligent machines live and work together. In this world, computerized robots would do jobs too dangerous or mundane for humans and assist in medicine to help people live longer. Whatever the future problems, math and computer scientists will work to find the solutions!

Robotics applications extend to soccer-playing models that have competed at the annual RoboCup since 1997.

TRY IT OUT! Ask a random group of 23 students from your school when their birthdays are. Scientists say there is a 50 percent chance that two of them will share the same birthday! What do your results say?

acoustical: related to the production or control of sound

algorithm: a series of steps followed in mathematical calculations or a problem-solving process to be completed by a computer

cyberattacks: attempts to take over, damage, or destroy a computer through unauthorized access

econophysics: a discipline that applies physics to the study of economics

hypothesize: to make an educated guess; to suggest an explanation based on a limited amount of evidence

licensed: obtained government permission showing ownership or official rights to do specific things

patent: a government-issued license that protects an invention from being copied by others

scientific method: a step-by-step method of research that includes making observations, forming hypotheses, performing experiments, and analyzing results

storyboarding: organizing illustrations or images in a sequence to visually pre-show how a movie, animation, or other type of media might look before it is completed

theorems: results that have been proven to be true from other sources

transistors: small devices that allow for the flow of electricity in computers and radios

trigonometry: a branch of mathematics that calculates lengths and angles of triangles

Baigrie, Brian S., ed. *History of Modern Science and Mathematics.* New York: Scribner's, 2002.

Blumenthal, Karen. *Steve Jobs: The Man Who Thought Different.* New York: Feiwel and Friends, 2012.

Bowden, Mark. *Worm: The First Digital World War.* New York: Atlantic Monthly Press, 2011.

Clawson, Calvin C. *The Mathematical Traveler: Exploring the Grand History of Numbers.* New York: Plenum, 1994.

Ifrah, Georges. *The Universal History of Computing: From the Abacus to the Quantum Computer.* New York: Wiley, 2001.

Moschovitis, Christos J. P., Hilary Poole, Tami Schuyler, and Theresa M. Senft. *History of the Internet: A Chronology, 1843 to the Present.* Santa Barbara, Calif.: ABC-CLIO, 1999.

Price, David A. *The Pixar Touch: The Making of a Company.* New York: Knopf, 2008.

Swade, Doron. *The Difference Engine: Charles Babbage and the Quest to Build the First Computer.* New York: Viking, 2001.

COOL MATH 4 KIDS

http://www.coolmath4kids.com/

This is an interactive math game website for kids, covering addition to geometry.

CRYPTOKIDS

http://www.nsa.gov/kids/home.shtml

On this website, kids can learn to make and decipher codes they design.

Note: Every effort has been made to ensure that the websites listed above are suitable for children, that they have educational value, and that they contain no inappropriate material. However, because of the nature of the Internet, it is impossible to guarantee that these sites will remain active indefinitely or that their contents will not be altered.